HOW TO RAISE AND TRAIN A
POMERANIAN

By ARTHUR LIEBERS
and
MRS. GEORGIE SHEPPARD

Distributed in the U.S.A. by T.F.H. Publications, Inc., 211 West Sylvania Avenue, P.O. Box 27, Neptune City, N.J. 07753; in England by T.F.H. (Gt. Britain) Ltd., 13 Nutley Lane, Reigate, Surrey; in Canada to the book store and library trade by Clarke, Irwin & Company, Clarwin House, 791 St. Clair Avenue West, Toronto 10, Ontario; in Canada to the pet trade by Rolf C. Hagen Ltd., 3225 Sartelon Street, Montreal 382, Quebec; in Southeast Asia by Y.W. Ong, 9 Lorong 36 Geylang, Singapore 14; in Australia and the south Pacific by Pet Imports Pty. Ltd., P.O. Box 149, Brookvale 2100, N.S.W., Australia. Published by T.F.H. Publications, Inc. Ltd., The British Crown Colony of Hong Kong.

ACKNOWLEDGMENTS

Pictures were taken by Heyer of Three Lions, Inc., with the cooperation of Mrs. Georgie M. Sheppard, Georgian Farm, Basking Ridge, New Jersey

Manufactured in the United States of America
Library of Congress Catalog Card No.: 59-9007

ISBN 0-87666-352-8

Contents

Intelligent, playful, alert and loyal—the Pom has all the traits of a delightful pet.

1. History of the Breed

The delicate looking Pomeranian is really a sled dog in miniature! If you feel the coat of an adult Pomeranian, you'll find that he has a double coat—a fluffy inner coat, the canine equivalent of winter underwear, and a looser long-haired outer coat. That's the same type of coat that protects the Husky and Samoyed who sleep outdoors through the Arctic winters. Stand a Pom next to one of the "sled dog" breeds and you'll see the remarkable facial and body resemblance.

The Pom's history goes back to the powerful sled dogs of Lapland and Iceland, which were eventually brought into Europe and bred with other dogs. The offspring, much larger than today's Poms, were used to herd sheep. With continued breeding, the size decreased, but even one hundred years ago Poms weighed as much as 30 pounds.

The dog gets his name from the German province of Pomerania. It was there that breeders realized what a delightful house pet the Pom would make, and started the process of breeding down to size. At the same time they improved the coat. From Germany, the dogs were brought to England where they soon became popular. Selective breeding continued, and today's Pom, the product of many generations of breeding, is one of the most popular "toy" breeds. Even today improvement continues, with the American Pomeranian Club encouraging selective breeding that will produce dogs that come as close as possible to the breed's standard.

POMERANIAN CHARACTERISTICS

The Pom is a delightful and active pet—playful, intelligent, courageous and loyal, although some are not especially "cuddly." Even an adult Pom seldom loses his pleasure in playing with his toys. As a watchdog, the Pom can hold his own. He greets any intruder with loud, sharp barks and dances out of reach until the family is aroused.

The Pom gets along well with other family pets. He will soon be eating out of the same dish as the family cat—if the cat is sociable—and he will put on a great show of wanting to tangle with the largest dogs in the neighborhood.

If possible, get a pair of Pomeranians. Two little dogs are no more demanding of care and food than one, and a pair of Poms will have more fun and provide more fun for you.

Your Pom will expect to be the center of attention. If he is ignored, he will put on a performance until he gets the attention he wants.

GOOD FOR CITY OR COUNTRY

The Pomeranian is well adapted to life in the city. His natural activity will give him enough exercise, even without frequent outings. The advantages of a dog that can be popped into a carrying case cannot be overestimated in a city with all its "No Dogs Allowed" signs.

Three Poms are three times as much fun as one, but not three times as much work.

Some Poms may snap when they are handled roughly, so be sure that children are gentle and kind.

At the same time, the Pom retains a strong hunting instinct from his wild ancestors. Let loose in a field where there are rabbits, he will take off in flight, and can often keep up with a full-grown rabbit. He seems to realize that he can't do anything if he does catch it, but he still keeps after his quarry until the rabbit disappears into a hole.

A NOTE OF CAUTION

Unfortunately, many Poms don't mix with small children. A child often thinks of a dog as a toy, and the Pom's "clutchy" coat makes him tempting to grab. If the child takes hold of the coat and won't let go, too, the dog often becomes agitated and snaps. Because of his light bone structure, too, the Pom cannot take the abuse that is the usual fate of the small dog around young children. Many responsible breeders refuse to sell a puppy to a family with young offspring, so if you have youngsters, you'd better wait until they're in their teens before bringing a Pom into the family.

STANDARDS OF THE BREED

The standards which have been adopted by the American Pomeranian Club and approved by the American Kennel Club set the present-day ideal for which Pom breeders are aiming. It is by these standards that the dog is judged in the show ring. However, even the most perfect specimen falls short of the standard in some respect. It's also impossible, even for a breeder or veterinarian, to tell how a puppy will shape up as an adult dog. The chances are that he will inherit the qualities for which his father and mother—or sire and dam in dog language—were bred, and if both his parents and grandparents had good show records he may have excellent possibilities. But until he's about six months old, he's still developing. At about a year, he will have his final conformation and coat.

Here, then, are the standards.

GENERAL APPEARANCE: The Pomeranian in build and appearance should be a compact, short-coupled dog, well-knit in frame. He should exhibit great intelligence in his expression, docility in his disposition, and activity and buoyancy in his deportment; he should be sound in action.

HEAD: The head should be wedge-shaped, somewhat foxy in outline, the skull being slightly flat, large in proportion to the muzzle. Its profile has a little stop (space between top of skull and muzzle) which must not be too pronounced, and hair on the face must be smooth or short-coated. The muzzle should finish rather fine. The teeth should meet in a scissors grip, in which part of the inner surface of the upper teeth meets and engages part of the outer surface of the lower teeth. This type of bite gives a firmer grip than one in which the edges of the teeth meet directly, and is subject to less wear. The mouth is considered *overshot* when the lower teeth fail to engage the inner surfaces of the upper teeth. The mouth is *undershot* when the lower teeth protrude beyond the upper teeth. One tooth out of line does not mean an undershot or overshot mouth.

EYES: The eyes should be medium in size, rather oblique in shape, not set too far apart or too close together, bright and dark in color. The eye rims of the blues and browns are self-colored. In all other colors the eye rims must be black.

EARS: The ears should be small, not set too far apart or too low down, and carried perfectly erect. They should be covered with soft, short hair. Trimming unruly hairs on edges of ears is permissible.

NOSE: The nose should be self-colored in blues and browns. In all other colors it should be black.

NECK AND SHOULDERS: The neck should be rather short, well set in and lion-like, covered with a profuse mane and frill of long, straight hair sweeping from the underjaw and covering the whole front part of the shoulders and chest as well as the top part of the shoulders. The shoulders must be clean and laid well back.

BODY: The back must be short and level, and the body compact, well-ribbed and rounded. The chest must be fairly deep.

LEGS: The forelegs must be well feathered and perfectly straight, of medium length and strength in due proportion to a well-balanced frame. The feet should be small, compact in shape, standing well up on the toes. The hind legs and thighs must be well feathered down to the hocks, and must be fine in bone and free in action. Trimming around the edges of the toes up the back of the legs to the first joint is permissible.

TAIL: The tail is characteristic of the breed and should be turned over the back and carried flat, set high. It must be profusely covered with long, spreading hair.

COAT: The Pomeranian must have two coats, an undercoat and an overcoat. The first is a soft, fluffy undercoat and the other a long, perfectly straight and glistening coat covering the whole body. It should be very abundant around the neck and forepart of the shoulders and chest where it should form a frill of profuse, standing-off straight hair extending over the shoulders. The hindquarters should be covered with long hair or feathering from top rump to the hocks. The texture of the guard hairs should be harsh to the touch.

COLOR: The following colors are permissible and recognized: black, brown, chocolate, red, orange, cream, orange-sable, wolf-sable, beaver, blue, white and parti-color. The parti-colored dogs are white with orange or black distributed on the body in even patches, and a white blaze is preferable. In mixed classes where whole-colored and parti-colored Pomeranians compete together, the preference should be given to the whole-colored specimens if in other points they are equal. Sables must be shaded throughout with three or more colors as uniformly as possible, with no patches of self-color, the undercoat being a light tan color, with deeper orange guard hairs ending in black tipping. Oranges must be self-colored throughout, with light shadings and no breeching.

SIZE: The weight of a Pomeranian for exhibition is 3 pounds to 7 pounds. The ideal size for show specimens is from 4 to 5 pounds.

CLASSIFICATION: The classes for Pomeranians may be divided by color in open classes as follows: black and brown; red, orange or cream; sables; any other allowable color.

Major Faults: Round, domey skull. Too large ears. Undershot. Pink eye rims. Light or Dudley (flesh-colored) nose. Out at elbows or shoulders. Flat sides. Down in pasterns. Cowhock. Soft, flat, open coat. Whole-colored dogs with white chest or white foot or leg. Black mask on an orange dog.

9

Objectionable: Overshot. Large, round or light eyes. High or low on legs. Trimming too close to time of show. Tail set too low on rump. Black, brown, blue or sable should be free of white hairs. Whites should be free of lemon or any other color. Black and tan. Underweight or overweight.

Minor Faults: Lippiness. Wide chest. Tail that curls back. Black mask on sable; white shadings on orange.

Your Pom will respond to affectionate play if children are taught to refrain from pulling and tugging his coat.

2. Selecting Your Pomeranian Puppy

Whether you are buying a Pomeranian for a pet or with hopes of someday walking in the show ring, you have to be cautious. Because of the popularity of these small dogs, unscrupulous breeders have been selling inferior dogs, puppies with distemper and, in some cases, crossbreeds. You may be able to get a good Pom for as little as $35, but the odds are against it. Generally you should be prepared to spend about $75 for a worth-while puppy, more if you are after a dog with highly desirable bloodlines and a number of champions in his lineage.

THE PUPPY'S PAPERS

If you are investing in a purebred dog, obtain the necessary papers from the seller, especially if you are planning to show or breed your dog. Usually the litter will have been registered with the American Kennel Club. This is necessary before the individual puppy can be registered. The breeder should provide you with an Application for Registration signed by the owner of the puppy's mother. Then you select a name for your dog (it must be 25 letters or less, and cannot duplicate the name of another dog of the breed, or be the name of a living person without his written permission). Enter the selected name on the form, fill in the blanks that make you the owner of record, and send it to the American Kennel Club, 221 Fourth Avenue, New York, N. Y., with the required fee. In a few weeks if all is in order you will receive the blue and white Certificate of Registration with your dog's stud book number.

THE PEDIGREE

The pedigree of your dog is a tracing of his family tree. Often the breeder will have the pedigree of the dog's dam and sire and may make out a copy for you. Or, you can write to the American Kennel Club once your dog has been registered and ask for a pedigree. The fee depends on how many generations back you want the pedigree traced. In addition to giving the immediate ancestors of your dog, the pedigree will show whether there

It's a difficult choice when you're faced with several fluffy, bright-eyed Poms. Health is the most important consideration.

are any champions or dogs that have won obedience degrees in his lineage. If you are planning selective breeding, the pedigree is also helpful to enable you to find other Poms that have the same general family background.

A HEALTHY PUPPY

The healthy puppy will be active, gay and alert, with bright, shiny eyes. He should not have running eyes or nose. At the age of six to eight weeks, when puppies are usually offered for sale, the Pom should look like a fluffy ball. While you may want a small dog, be wary of taking the "runt" of the litter as there may be some physical reason for his small size. In buying a puppy—especially a higher-priced one—it is always wise to make your purchase subject to the approval of a veterinarian. The seller will usually allow you eight hours in which to take the puppy to a vet to have his health checked. However, come to a clear agreement on what happens if the vet rejects the puppy. It should be understood whether rejection means that you get your money back or merely choice of another puppy from the same litter.

MALE OR FEMALE?

Unless you want to breed your pet and raise a litter of puppies it doesn't matter whether you choose a male or female. Both sexes are pretty much the same in disposition and character, and both make equally good pets.

If you choose a female but decide you don't want to raise puppies, your dog can be spayed and will remain a healthy, lively pet.

ADULT OR PUP?

Whether to buy a grown dog or a small puppy is another question. It is undeniably fun to watch your dog grow all the way from a baby, sprawling and playful, to a mature, dignified dog. If you don't have the time to spend on the more frequent meals, housebreaking, and other training a puppy needs in order to become a dog you can be proud of, then choose an older, partly trained pup or a grown dog. If you want a show dog, remember that no one, not even an expert, can predict with 100% accuracy what a small puppy will be when he grows up.

WORMING AND INOCULATION

Before you take your puppy home, find out from the breeder if he has already been wormed or inoculated for distemper and rabies. Practically all puppies will have worms which they acquire from eating worm eggs, from fleas, or from their mother. The breeder usually gives the puppies a worming before he sells them. If yours has already been wormed, find out when and what treatment was given. The breeder may be able to advise you on any further treatment that is necessary. While there are many commercial worming preparations on the market, it's generally safer to let the vet handle it. There will be more about worms in Chapter 3.

If your puppy has been inoculated against distemper, you will also have to know when this was done so you can give the information to your vet. He will complete the series of shots. If your puppy has not yet been given this protection, your vet should take care of it immediately. Distemper is highly prevalent and contagious. Don't let your puppy out of doors until he has had his distemper shots and they have had time to take effect.

As a rule, kennels and breeders do not inoculate puppies against rabies. In some areas, rabies inoculation is required by law. However, the possibility of your dog becoming affected with rabies, a contact disease, is very slight in most parts of the country. To be perfectly safe, check with your vet who will be familiar with the local ordinances and will advise you.

While the distemper inoculation is permanent and can be supplemented by "booster" shots, rabies inoculation must be repeated yearly. When your puppy receives it, the vet will give you a tag for the dog's collar certifying that he has received the protection. He will also give you a certificate for your own records. For foreign travel and some interstate travel, rabies inoculation is required.

3. Caring For Your Pomeranian

BRINGING YOUR PUPPY HOME

When you bring your puppy home, remember that he is used to the peace and relative calm of a life of sleeping, eating and playing with his brothers and sisters. The trip away from all this is an adventure in itself, and so is adapting to a new home. So let him take it easy for a while. Don't let the whole neighborhood pat and poke him at one time. Be particularly careful when children want to handle him, for they cannot understand the difference between the delicate living puppy and the toy dog they play with and maul.

THE PUPPY'S BED

It is up to you to decide where the puppy will sleep. He should have his own place, and not be allowed to climb all over the furniture. He should sleep out of drafts, but not right next to the heat, which would make him too sensitive to the cold when he goes outside.

You might partition off a section of a room — the kitchen is good because it's usually warm and he'll have some companionship there. Set up some sort of low partition that he can't climb, give him a pillow or old blanket for his bed and cover the floor with a thick layer of newspapers. If he seems a bit timid or retiring, get a sturdy cardboard box, cut a large door in one side and put his bed in there. Since he will need some exercise, he should have about four feet of roaming area.

You have already decided where the puppy will sleep before you bring him home. Let him stay there, or in the corner he will soon learn is "his," most of the time, so that he will gain a sense of security from the familiar. Give the puppy a little food when he arrives, but don't worry if he isn't hungry at first. He will soon develop an appetite when he grows accustomed to his surroundings. The first night the puppy may cry a bit from lonesomeness, but if he has an old blanket or rug to curl up in he will be cozy. In winter a hot water bottle will help replace the warmth of his littermates, or the ticking of a clock may provide company.

FEEDING THE PUPPY

By the time a puppy is eight weeks old, he should be fully weaned and eating from a dish. Always find out what the seller has been feeding the puppy as it is well to keep him on the same diet for a while. Any sudden change in a puppy's feeding habits may cause loose bowels or constipation.

Common sense is your best guide to feeding your Pomeranian puppy properly. Until he is about two months old, the puppy should be fed four times daily; until he is four months old, three times; from four months to a year, twice; and after a year, he should manage nicely on one feeding a day.

How much food each time? Roughly, about an ounce of food per pound of puppy at each meal. However, if yours acts hungry, add a bit more to his dish; if he snubs a meal, just take it away and don't offer him any food until his next feeding time. As to what to feed the puppy, you have a wide choice. Fresh beef or meat is probably the best food, but don't get the more expensive leaner cuts of meat. The lower-priced hamburger grind at your butcher or the supermarket contains a lot of fat that your dog needs in his diet. The needle-like teeth of the Pom are for biting, not chewing, so his food should be ground or cut into tiny bits. If you buy canned dog food, study the label carefully and make certain that it contains a large proportion of meat. Many kennels feed their dogs exclusively on kibble — the broken-biscuit type of dog food or the meal that comes in bags or cardboard containers. If you feed the

Your Pom should have his own warm, draft-free bed. A cardboard box, lined with a pillow or blanket, is a better idea than the wicker bed which the puppy may chew.

dried food, add some beef fat or bacon drippings occasionally. On almost all packages of food you'll find the feeding directions for puppies and adult dogs and you won't go wrong if you follow them. However, there is a big difference in the quality of canned dog foods — the higher-priced cans usually contain much more actual meat than the lower-priced.

In addition to the basic food, you should give your dog an occasional egg (scrambled or hard-boiled), cottage cheese, green vegetables or grated carrot, and cod-liver oil, wheat germ or vitamin supplement. But don't make the mistake of coddling him and stuffing him with every vitamin and food supplement on the market. If you find that your puppy or older dog persistently refuses a certain food, don't force him to eat it. He may know best.

The puppy's food should be served at room temperature, never hot or cold. And of course you won't let your dog near chicken bones or fish with bones that can catch in his throat or tear his intestines. Don't feed him pork, fried meats or over-spiced foods either.

According to the latest research on dog nutrition, cow's milk is not a desirable dog food. It differs considerably from the mother dog's milk and many dogs are unable to get much benefit from it. In addition, many puppies develop loose bowels from cow's milk.

If you are using a food that has to be mixed with a liquid, use luke-warm water or any bland soup rather than milk. Keep in mind that your dog's digestive system is more like a wolf's than a human baby's. Your tiny dog needs the same foods that a German Shepherd or a Boxer needs, just less in quantity.

WATCHING THE PUPPY'S HEALTH

The first step in protecting the health of your puppy is a visit to the veterinarian. If the breeder has not given your puppy his first distemper shots, have your vet do it. You should also have your Pom protected against hepatitis, and, if required by local law or if your vet suggests it, against rabies. Your puppy should receive his full quota of protective inoculations, especially if you plan to show him later. Select a veterinarian you feel you can trust and keep his phone number handy. Any vet will be glad to give a regular "patient" advice over the phone — often without charge.

Occasional loose bowels in a puppy generally isn't anything too serious. It can be the result of an upset stomach or a slight cold. Sometimes it will clear up in a day or so without any treatment. If you want to help the puppy's digestion, add some cottage cheese to his diet, or give him a few drops of kaopectate. Instead of tap water, give him barley or oatmeal water (just as you would a human baby). However, if the looseness persists for more than a day or two, a visit to the vet may be required. If the puppy has normal bowel movements alternating with loose bowel movements, it may be a symptom of worms.

If the puppy upchucks a meal or vomits up slime or white froth, it may indicate that his stomach is upset. One good stomach-settler is a pinch of baking soda, or about 8 or 10 drops of pure witch hazel in a teaspoon of cold water two or three times a day. In case of vomiting you should skip a few meals to give the stomach a chance to clear itself out. When you start to feed him again, give him cooked scraped beef for his first meals and then return to his normal diet. Persistent vomiting may indicate a serious stomach upset or even poisoning and calls for professional help.

The Pom is more subject to gastritis and enteritis—inflammation of the mucous membrane of the stomach or intestine—than many other breeds. This may be because of the thin coat of hair on his belly compared to his heavy upper coat. Symptoms are repeated vomiting of slime, froth or mucus, coupled with excessive thirst and lack of appetite. The disease can appear quickly, so it is a good idea to get a remedy from your vet and keep it on hand.

WORMING

Practically all puppies start out in life with worms in their insides, either acquired from the mother or picked up in their sleeping quarters. However, there are six different types of worms. Some will be visible in the stool as small white objects; others require microscopic examination of the stool for identification. While there are many commercial worm remedies on the market, it is safest to leave that to your veterinarian, and to follow his instructions on feeding the puppy before and after the worming. If you find that you must administer a worm remedy yourself, read the directions carefully and administer the smallest possible dose. Keep the puppy confined after treatment for worms, since many of the remedies have a strong laxative action and the puppy will soil the house if allowed to roam freely.

THE USEFUL THERMOMETER

Almost every serious puppy ailment shows itself by an increase in the puppy's body temperature. If your little Pom acts lifeless, looks dull-eyed and gives an impression of illness, check by using a rectal thermometer. Hold the dog, insert the thermometer which has been lubricated with vaseline and take a reading. The normal temperature is 100.6 to 101.5 (higher than the normal human temperature). Excitement may send it up slightly, but any rise of more than a few points is cause for alarm.

DON'T LET HIM JUMP

Despite his small size, the Pomeranian is not an especially delicate dog. However, he does have light bones and shallow joint sockets, and can injure himself if he jumps from any height. Try to keep your Pom from injuring himself. If you detect a limp or awkward movements of a limb, check with your vet. If, for any reason, you cannot, try heat treatment on the affected area and gentle massage. Don't use liniments, which may be poisonous to the dog if he licks his coat. Dislocations at the joint are fairly common Pom accidents and call for resetting by a vet.

Puppies need sunshine and fresh air as much as children do, but they shouldn't be allowed outside until they have had all their protective inoculations.

SOME CANINE DISEASES

You should be familiar with the symptoms of some of the more prevalent canine diseases which can strike your dog.

COUGHS, COLDS, BRONCHITIS, PNEUMONIA

Respiratory diseases may affect the Pom because he is forced to live in a human rather than a natural doggy environment. Being subjected to a draft or cold after a bath, sleeping near an air conditioner or in the path of air from a fan or near a hot air register or radiator can cause one of these respiratory ailments. The symptoms are similar to those in humans. However, the germs of these diseases are different and do not affect both dogs and humans so that they cannot catch them from each other. Treatment is pretty much the same as for a child with the same illness. Keep the puppy warm, quiet, well fed. Your veterinarian has antibiotics and other remedies to help the pup fight back.

Don't make the common mistake of running your dog to the vet every time he sneezes. If he seems to have a light cold, give him about a quarter of an aspirin tablet and see that he doesn't overexercise himself.

MAJOR DISEASES OF THE DOG

With the proper series of inoculations, your Pomeranian will be almost completely protected against the following canine diseases. However, it occasionally happens that the shot doesn't take and sometimes a different form of the virus appears against which your dog may not be protected.

Rabies: This is an acute disease of the dog's central nervous system and is spread by the bite of an infected animal, the saliva carrying the infection. Rabies occurs in two forms. The first is "Furious Rabies" in which the dog shows a period of melancholy or depression, then irritation, and finally paralysis. The first period lasts from a few hours to several days. During this time, the dog is cross and will try to hide from members of the family. He appears restless and will change his position often. He loses his appetite for food and begins to lick, bite and swallow foreign objects. During the "irritation" phase the dog is spasmodically wild and has impulses to run away. He acts in a fearless manner and runs and bites at everything in sight. If he is caged or confined he will fight at the bars, often breaking teeth or fracturing his jaw. His bark becomes a peculiar howl. In the final or paralysis stage, the animal's lower jaw becomes paralyzed and hangs down; he walks with a stagger and saliva drips from his mouth. Within four to eight days after the onset of paralysis, the dog dies.

The second form of rabies, "Dumb Rabies," is characterized by the dog's walking in a bear-like manner with his head down. The lower jaw is paralyzed and the dog is unable to bite. Outwardly it may seem as though he has a bone caught in his throat.

Even if your Pom should be bitten by a rabid dog or other animal, he can probably be saved if you get him to the vet in time for a series of injections. However, by the time the symptoms appear the disease is so far advanced that no cure is possible. But remember that an annual rabies inoculation is almost certain protection against rabies.

Distemper: Young dogs are most susceptible to distemper, although it may affect dogs of all ages. The dog will lose his appetite, seem depressed, chilled, and run a fever. Often he will have a watery discharge from his eyes and nose. Unless treated promptly, the disease goes into advanced stages with infections of the lungs, intestines and nervous system, and dogs that recover may be left with some impairment such as a twitch or other nervous mannerism. The best protection against this is very early inoculation — preferably even before the puppy is old enough to go out into the street and meet other dogs.

Hepatitis: Veterinarians report an increase in the spread of this virus disease in recent years, usually with younger dogs as the victims. The initial symptoms — drowsiness, vomiting, great thirst, loss of appetite and a high temperature — closely resemble distemper. These symptoms are often accompanied by swellings on the head, neck and lower parts of the belly. The disease strikes quickly and death may occur in a few hours. Protection is afforded by injection with a new vaccine.

Leptospirosis: This disease is caused by bacteria which live in stagnant or slow-moving water. It is carried by rats and dogs, and many dogs are believed to get it from licking the urine or feces of infected rats. The symptoms are increased thirst, depression and weakness. In the acute stage, there is vomiting, diarrhea and a brown discoloration of the jaws, tongue and teeth, caused by an inflammation of the kidneys. This disease can be cured if caught in time, but it is best to ward it off with a vaccine which your vet can administer along with the distemper shots.

External Parasites: The Pomeranian needs special care in regard to fleas, ticks or lice. Scratching at the irritation caused by these pests can ruin the dog's coat. The dog that is groomed regularly and provided with clean sleeping quarters should not have much trouble on this score. However, it would be a wise precaution to spray his sleeping quarters occasionally with an anti-parasite powder that you can get at your pet shop or from your vet. For the dog himself, because of his luxuriant coat, a liquid spray would probably be more effective than a powder. If the dog is out of doors during the tick season he should be treated with a dip-bath.

Skin Ailments: It may be difficult to spot skin disorders on your long-haired Pomeranian, but any persistent scratching may indicate an irritation, and whenever you groom him, look for the reddish spots that may indicate eczema or some rash or fungus infection. Rather than self-treatment, take him to the veterinarian as some of the conditions may be difficult to eradicate and can cause permanent harm to his coat.

FIRST AID FOR YOUR DOG

In general, a dog will lick his cuts and wounds and they'll heal. If he swallows anything harmful, chances are he'll throw it up. But it will probably make you feel better to help him if he's hurt, so treat his wounds as you would your own. Wash out the dirt and apply an antiseptic or ointment. If you put on a bandage, you'll have to do something to keep the dog from trying to remove it. A large cardboard ruff around his neck will prevent him from licking his chest or body. You can tape up his nails to keep him from scratching, or make a "bootie" for his paws.

If you think your dog has a broken bone, before moving him apply a splint just as you would to a person's limb. If there is bleeding that won't stop, apply a tourniquet between the wound and heart, but loosen it every few minutes to prevent damage to the circulatory system.

If you are afraid that your dog has swallowed poison and you can't get the vet fast enough, try to induce vomiting by giving him a strong solution of salt water or mustard in water.

SOME "BUTS"

First, don't be frightened by the number of diseases a dog can get. The majority of dogs never get any of them. If you need assurance, look at any book on human diseases. How many have you had?

Don't become a dog-hypochondriac. Veterinarians have enough work taking care of sick dogs and doing preventive work with their patients. Don't rush your pet to the vet every time he sneezes or seems tired. All dogs have days on which they feel lazy and want to lie around doing nothing.

THE FEMALE PUPPY

If you want to spay your female you can have it done while she is still a puppy. Her first seasonal period will probably occur between eight and ten months, although it may be as early as six or delayed until she is a year old. She may be spayed before or after this, or you may breed her (at a later season) and still spay her afterward.

The first sign of the female's being in season is a thin red discharge, which will increase for about a week, when it changes color to a thin yellowish stain, lasting about another week. Simultaneously there is a swelling of the vulva, the dog's external sexual organ. The second week is the crucial period, when she could be bred if you wanted her to have puppies, but it is possible for the period to be shorter or longer, so it is best not to take unnecessary risks at any time. After a third week the swelling decreases and the period is over for about six months.

If you have an absolutely climb-proof and dig-proof run within your yard, it will be safe to leave her there, but otherwise the female in season should be shut indoors. Don't leave her out alone for even a minute; she should be exercised only on leash. If you want to prevent the neighborhood dogs from hanging around your doorstep, as they inevitably will as soon as they discover that your female is in season, take her some distance away from the house before you let her relieve herself. Take her to a nearby park or field in the car for a chance to stretch her legs. After the three weeks are up you can let her out as before, with no worry that she can have puppies until the next season. But if you want to have her spayed, consult your veterinarian about the time and age at which he prefers to do it. With a young dog the operation is simple and after a night or two at the animal hospital she can be at home, wearing only a small bandage as a souvenir.

4. Grooming Your Pomeranian

At times during his puppyhood, your Pom will not look like a Pom because of the changes in his coat. Don't panic and assume that he is ill or not a purebred dog at all. The change is natural. Here is the coat schedule of the young Pomeranian, although the stages may vary, depending on the individual dog, the time of year and other factors.

Two months: Coat should be long and fluffy, extending to the point of the ears.

Three months: Coat becomes ragged.

Four-five months: Puppy coat will shed, so that the puppy is often short-haired for several weeks.

Six months: Coat again becomes fluffy.

About ten months: Puppy should have double coat with heavy, stand-off outer coat. The full adult coat may not develop until the dog is three or four years old.

CARING FOR THE COAT

From an early age, your Pom should be accustomed to being handled. You will both be more comfortable during grooming sessions if he learns to jump up on a bench or table for his beauty treatments.

It is not necessary to bathe your puppy or grown dog unless he gets himself thoroughly dirty. With a little care, daily brushing and weekly cleaning, many Poms go through life with nary a bath. Too frequent bathing removes the oil from the coat and skin and leaves the coat soft and lifeless.

A wide-toothed comb, blunt-end scissors, brush (bristle is better than nylon) and sponge are all the tools you'll need. Use the scissors to clip the long hairs above, below and on the sides of his anus. The sponge is for removing particles of food from his face after each meal and occasionally cleaning the hairs on his backside. Usually a Pomeranian is not as dirty as he may look. His dense inner coat keeps his skin clean even though his outer coat is covered with dirt, and sponging will make him look respectable again. Use the comb only when you find tangles or mats in the outer coat, and be careful not to pull hard. If neglected, mats will have to be cut off, seriously impairing the coat.

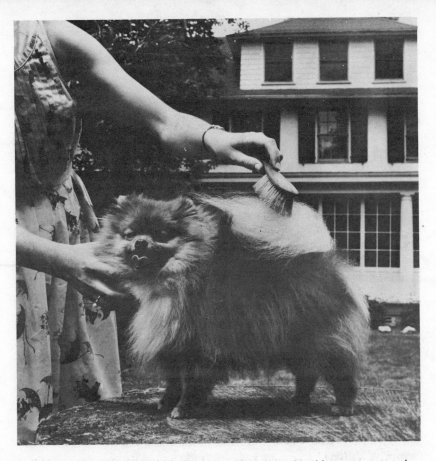

The Pom's beautiful coat needs grooming, and it is no trouble if he gets accustomed to it from puppyhood and it becomes part of his daily routine.

DAILY GROOMING ROUTINE

After his morning run, place the Pom on the table and wipe his eyes and stomach with the damp sponge. Then give him a brisk brushing. When you brush him, especially during the summer and fall months, check his coat for any sign of fleas, lice or ticks. If you do find parasites, use a spray or dip to get rid of them. When there are fleas, you will also have to change the dog's bedding and spray the areas of the house where he stays, paying special attention to cracks in the floor and along the baseboards. Repeat the de-fleaing treatment in about a week. Make sure the puppy doesn't lick too much insecticide off his coat; if necessary, you can put a clown collar around his neck so he won't be able to reach his body with his tongue. Don't leave the flea powder on too long, as it may be strong enough to burn his skin or coat.

Examine your Pom's coat and skin every day. Ruffle up his inner coat to see if any parasites are present.

If you find ticks, be sure to remove the entire insects. You can touch them with a drop of iodine or a lighted cigarette (be careful not to burn the dog) to break their grip. Then lift them off, one at a time, with a pair of tweezers or a tissue and burn them or drop them into kerosene or gasoline to kill them.

WEEKLY GROOMING ROUTINE

If you can spare the time and want your Pom to look his best, a weekly trimming is called for. If possible, have someone with experience show you how to do, this before trying it yourself. If you can't get professional help, put your Pom up on the table, take a deep breath and start.

Lay the tail flat against the back and trim the hair close to the roof of the tail. Cut off any short, straggly hairs and clip away the longer hairs near the anus. Then drop the tail and get down to the paws. They should have the appearance of a cat's paws, round and neat, with no stray hairs evident. Leave the short hairs on the front of the legs alone, but cut the hairs on the sides and backs of the legs to an even length. Next step—the ears, which require a bit of fancy barbering. Hold the ear tip carefully to avoid cutting the skin. Leave about ¼ inch of hair on the inside edge of the ear (toward the head), about ½ inch on the outside edge. Trim the head hairs to avoid a straggly appearance and clip the whiskers. If this job seems too formidable, you can have it done professionally or skip it entirely.

A good sponging with shampoo comes next, concentrating on the stomach and rear. Then wipe dry with a soft towel. Afterward, apply a grooming preparation, working it in with your fingertips. Then brush gently but thoroughly to remove dead hairs in order to make room for new, live hairs to push through.

A well-groomed Pom is a delight to behold, and even he will be proud of his appearance.

Clip your Pom's toenails with a special clipper, being especially careful not to cut into the blood vessels. Your vet will show you how to do it.

WATCH THE TOENAILS

Many dogs that run on gravel or pavements keep their toenails down and seldom need clipping. But a dog that doesn't do much running, or runs on grass, will grow long toenails that can be harmful. The long nails will force the dog's toes into the air and spread his feet wide. In addition, the nails may force the dog into an unnatural stance that may produce lameness.

You can control your dog's toenails by cutting them with a special dog clipper or by filing them. Many dogs object to the clipping and it takes some experience to learn just how to do it without cutting into the blood vessels. Your vet will probably examine your dog's nails whenever you bring him in and will trim them at no extra charge. He can show you how to do it yourself in the future. If you prefer, you can file the points off your dog's nails every few weeks with a flat wooden file.

EYES, EARS AND TEETH

If you notice matter collecting in the corners of the dog's eyes, wipe it out with a piece of cotton or tissue.

If your Pom scratches at his ears or shakes his head, probe his ears very cautiously with a cotton swab dipped in mineral or castor oil. You may

Clip the straggly hairs from your Pom's paws so they look round and neat.

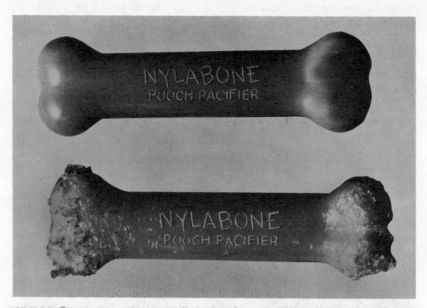

NYLABONE® is a necessity that is available at your local petshop (not in supermarkets). The puppy or grown dog chews the hambone flavored nylon into a frilly dog toothbrush, massaging his gums and cleaning his teeth as he plays. Veterinarians highly recommend this product . . . but beware of cheap imitations which might splinter or break.

find an accumulation of wax that will work itself out. Any signs of dirt or dried blood in the ears probably indicates ear mites or an infection and requires treatment by your vet. In the summer, especially when flies are heavy, the dog may have sore ears from fly bites. If that happens, wash his ears with warm water and a mild soap, cover with a mild ointment and try to keep him indoors until his ears have healed.

If you give your Pom a hard chewing bone—the kind you can buy at a pet store—it will serve him as your tooth brush serves you and will prevent the accumulation of tartar on his teeth. However, check his mouth occasionally and take him to the vet if you find collected tartar or bloody spots on his gums.

5. Housebreaking and Training Your Pomeranian

The first months of your Pom's life will be a busy time. While he's getting his preventive shots and becoming acquainted with his new family, he should learn the elements of housebreaking that will make him a welcome addition to your home and community.

HOUSEBREAKING THE POMERANIAN PUPPY

Housebreaking the puppy isn't difficult because his natural instinct is to keep the place where he sleeps and plays clean. The most important factor is to keep him confined to a fairly small area during the training period. You will find it almost impossible to housebreak a puppy who is given free run of the house. After months of yelling and screaming, you may finally get it through his head that the parlor rug is "verboten," but it will be a long, arduous process.

FIRST, PAPER TRAINING

Spread papers over the puppy's living area. Then watch him carefully. When you notice him starting to whimper, sniff the ground or run around in agitated little circles, rush him to the place that you want to serve as his "toilet" and hold him there till he does his business. Then praise him lavishly. When you remove the soiled papers, leave a small damp piece so that the puppy's sense of smell will lead him back there next time. If he makes a mistake, wash it immediately with warm water, followed by a rinse with water and vinegar. That will kill the odor and prevent discoloration.

It shouldn't take more than a few days for the puppy to get the idea of using newspaper. When he becomes fairly consistent, reduce the area of paper to a few sheets in a corner. As soon as you think he has the idea fixed in his mind, you can let him roam around the house a bit, but keep an eye on him. It might be best to keep him on leash the first few days so you can rush him back to his paper at any signs of an approaching accident.

The normally healthy puppy will want to relieve himself when he wakes up in the morning, after each feeding and after strenuous exercise.

To begin housebreaking, spread paper over the Pom's living area. As he learns what it's for, you can begin to reduce the paper-covered area, but don't be in a hurry to give him the run of the house.

During early puppyhood any excitement, such as the return home of a member of the family or the approach of a visitor, may result in floor-wetting, but that phase should pass in a few weeks.

OUTDOOR HOUSEBREAKING

Keep in mind during the housebreaking process that you can't expect too much from your puppy until he is about 5 months old. Before that, his muscles and digestive system just aren't under his control. However, you can begin outdoor training even while you are paper training the puppy. (He should have learned to walk on lead at this point. See page 37.) First thing in the morning, take him outdoors (to the curb if you are in a city) and walk him back and forth in a small area until he relieves himself. He will probably make a puddle and then just walk around uncertain of what is expected of him. You can try standing him over a piece of newspaper which may give him the idea. Some dog trainers use glycerine suppositories at this point for fast action. Praise the dog every time taking him outside brings results and he'll get the idea. After each meal take him to the same spot.

Use some training word to help your puppy learn. Pick a word that you won't use for any other command and repeat it while you are walking your dog in his outdoor "business" area. It will be a big help when the dog is older if you have some word of command that he can connect with approval to relieve himself in a strange place. You'll find, when you begin the outdoor training, that the male puppy usually requires a longer walk than the female. Both male and female puppies will squat. It isn't until he's quite a bit older that the male dog will begin to lift his leg.

NIGHTTIME TRAINING

If you hate to give up any sleep, you can train your Pomeranian puppy to go outdoors during the day and use the paper at night for the first few months. After he's older, he'll be able to contain himself all night and wait for his first morning walk. However, if you want to speed up the outdoor training so that you can leave the dog alone in the house with less fear of an accident, keep him confined at night so that he has enough room to move around in his bed but not enough to get any distance away from it. When he has to go, he'll whine loudly enough to attract your attention. Then take him or let him out. You may have to get up once or twice a night for a few weeks but then you can be fairly sure that your puppy will behave indoors — although accidents will happen. Sometimes even a grown dog will suddenly — and for no apparent reason — soil the house, usually the most expensive carpet in it.

Occasionally a puppy that seems to have been housebroken will revert to indiscriminate acts all over the place. If that happens it may be necessary to go back to the beginning and repeat the paper training.

Several puppies can eat together if you make sure each gets his share.

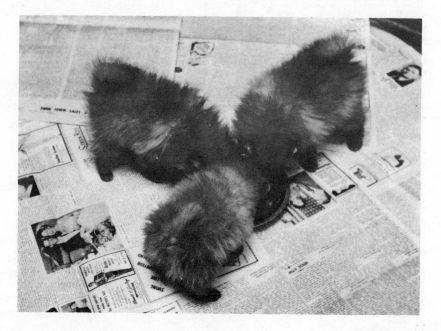

WHEN HE MISBEHAVES

Rubbing a puppy's nose in his dirt or whacking him with a newspaper may make you feel better, but it won't help train the puppy. A dog naturally *wants* to do the right thing for his master. Your job is to show him what you want. If an accident happens, ignore it unless you can catch him immediately and then in a firm tone express your displeasure and take him to the spot he should have used. A puppy has a short memory span, and bawling him out for something that happened a half hour before will have no meaning to him. When he does use the right place, be lavish with praise and petting, but first be sure he has finished. Many a puppy has left a trail of water across a floor because someone interrupted him to tell him how well he was doing.

PUPPY DISCIPLINE

A 6- or 8-week-old puppy is old enough to understand what is probably the most important word in his vocabulary—"NO!" The first time you see the puppy doing something he shouldn't do, chewing something he shouldn't chew or wandering in a forbidden area, it's time to teach him. Shout "No" and stamp your foot, hit the table with a piece of newspaper or make some other loud noise. Dogs, especially very young ones, don't like loud noises and your misbehaving pet will readily connect the word with something unpleasant. If he persists, repeat the "No," hold him firmly and slap him sharply across the nose. Before you protest to the A.S.P.C.A. you should realize that a dog does not resent being disciplined if he is doing something wrong and is caught in the act. However, do not chase a puppy around while waving a rolled-up newspaper at him or trying to swat him. Punish him only when you have a firm hold on him. Above all, never call him to you and then punish him. He must learn to associate coming to you with something pleasant.

Every puppy will pick things up. So the second command should be "Drop it!" or "Let go!" Don't engage in a tug-of-war with the puppy, but take the forbidden object from him even if you have to pry his jaws open with your fingers. Many dogs will release what they are holding if you just blow sharply into their faces. Let your dog know that you are displeased when he picks up something he shouldn't.

If you give him toys of his own, he will be less liable to chew your possessions. Avoid soft rubber toys that he can chew to pieces. A firm rubber ball or a tennis ball or a strong piece of leather is a good plaything. Don't give him cloth toys, as he'll probably swallow pieces and have trouble getting them out of his system. Skip the temptation to give him an old slipper, because it will be hard for him to distinguish between that and a brand-new pair you certainly won't want him to chew.

However, even with training, reconcile yourself to the fact that during puppyhood things will be chewed and damaged, but that's a passing phase in the growth of the dog.

Your Pom needs human companionship, but he must be taught to be quiet when left alone.

BARKING

Small dogs are characteristically "yappy." Perhaps they try to make up in sound what they lack in size, but with patience and persistence you can get your Pom to keep quiet even when he's left alone in the house or when a visitor rings the doorbell or the milkman comes.

Show the puppy from the start that you consider excessive barking an anti-social act. When he barks, grab his muzzle, hold his mouth closed and give him a firm command to stop. Above all, do not show him by your attitude that barking is "cute" sometimes, and then reprimand him for barking at another time. When the puppy barks, make a louder noise than he can and shout "No." When he finds that his bark brings an unpleasant and slightly frightening reaction, he'll stop barking.

Teaching the dog not to bark when he's left alone in the house calls for the application of canine psychology. Leave him alone in a room. When he barks, go back into the room and reprimand him severely, then step out again and wait by the door. He may bark as soon as he thinks you're gone. When that happens, pound the door with your fist and order him to stop. And don't think that training a dog not to bark will break his spirit.

Teach your pup that dogs and cars don't mix. If he begins to chase cars, put a quick stop to it.

Training the Pom not to bark at other dogs will take a bit of work on your part. The Pomeranian straining at his leash and barking his head off at a big Boxer or Collie makes a delightful picture, but it gets annoying if it goes on year after year. Be firm from the start. At the first sign of a bark at another dog, grab his muzzle and order him to stop. If he persists you can make a no-bark muzzle by taking a piece of gauze bandage, running it around his muzzle and under his jaws and knotting it around his neck. When you put it on, make it clear to the dog that it's being done because he's barking. After a few minutes take it off but put it back on if he barks again. He'll soon learn that barking gets his nose tied up and not-barking doesn't.

THE TOO-FRIENDLY PUPPY

Your Pom will probably like people and will try to show his liking for them by trying to climb all over anyone he meets. This may be another "cute" act, but if you're planning to show your dog, you won't want him climbing all over the judge in the ring. Besides, not all your friends and relatives are dog lovers and many people prefer to admire dogs from a slight distance. Curbing the puppy's desire to scramble over people will require cooperation from others. Instruct your friends to give the puppy a slight kick or slap when he gets overattentive, but then have them call him back and pet him to show that people aren't hostile.

And here's a tip on petting the puppy. If everyone pets him on top of the head, as most people do, he may develop the habit of coming over to people with his head down to receive his due. Instead, he should be chucked under the chin. That will keep him in an attractive head-up pose when he greets people — and improve his posture in the show ring or on the street.

Your Pom will keep his head up if you scratch him under the chin instead of on top of his head.

Plenty of grass to run on is fine, of course, but your Pom will be equally happy in a city apartment.

CLIMBING ON FURNITURE

Despite his short legs, your puppy may show a surprising ability to climb onto upholstered furniture. The upholstery holds the scent of the people he likes, and besides, it's more comfortable than the hard floor or even the carpet. Sometimes verbal corrections will be enough to establish the fact that the furniture is taboo. If not, try putting crinkly cellophane on the furniture to keep him off. If that doesn't work, you can get liquids at your pet store that you can't smell, but whose odor keeps the dog off. Another good trick is the mousetrap surprise. Put a small unbaited but set mousetrap on the piece of furniture that your Pomeranian chooses for his naps. Once he's surprised by the snap of the trap, he'll keep away from that spot. You can put the trap under a piece of paper or cloth if you're afraid that it may hurt the dog, or you may even find a child's toy that snaps which will serve the same purpose as the mousetrap.

WALKING ON LEAD

Now comes another battle of wills, when you train your Pomeranian to walk at the end of his leash — what the "doggy" people always call the "lead." For the Pom, the best type is the thin, nylon lead with a slip-noose collar arrangement that is called a show lead. This type of leash will give you enough control over the dog to manage him and it won't destroy the Pom's natural hairline.

First give the puppy a chance to get acquainted with the lead and collar. Slip the collar around his neck and let the lead dangle on the floor and let him play with it for a while to get the feel of it. Then pick up the end of the lead and call the dog over to you, giving the lead gentle jerks to get across the idea that he should move with the lead. You can expect a battle royal at first, as the puppy isn't giving up his freedom to roam without putting up a good fight. But lead-training is the basis of all further training, so you have to be firm enough to win.

Training to walk on lead will be easier if you hold the lead in your right hand, with your Pom at your left side. Use your left hand to snap the lead when corrections are necessary.

When you begin walking him outdoors you can expect him to pull back with all his strength, plant his hindquarters on the pavement or try to run in circles around you.

There are two important tricks in training the dog to follow the lead. First, do not pull the dog. Instead, use the lead to give *sharp jerks* and then release the pressure. The dog soon learns that if he follows the path of least resistance, his walks are pleasanter. Second, walk *fast* when you are training the dog to follow the lead. Walking at a brisk pace forces the dog to follow you; walking slowly gives him too much opportunity for antics of his own.

Use surprise tactics. If the dog runs to the end of the lead to bark at another dog, reverse your course sharply, giving the lead a snap to pull the dog back with you. You won't hurt him. However, limit the length of your first walks to a few minutes each. Another good idea is to carry the puppy a distance away from home and then put him down and start walking back home. Many young dogs are better at coming than they are at going. Keep the puppy at your left side when you are walking him. Hold the lead in your right hand, using your left hand to snap the lead for corrections. Keep up a running chain of conversation with the dog while he is on lead to keep his attention focused on you. Above all, don't give in too easily and pick him up. If he can, your Pom will outsmart you and turn you into his personal taxi. Don't let him!

As soon as your Pom begins to get the idea of the lead, you can begin his curb training, discussed on page 30.

6. Obedience Training for Your Pomeranian

The purpose of obedience training is not to turn your dog into a puppet — you can be sure this won't happen to your spirited Pom — but to make him a civilized member of the community in which he will live, and to keep him safe. As soon as your dog has been housebroken and has learned to walk fairly well on lead, you can gradually begin his more formal training. This training is most important as it makes the difference between having an undisciplined animal in the house or having an enjoyable companion. Both you and your dog will learn a lot from training. Although your Pom is a toy dog, he is more than a lap dog or showpiece. Poms have done very well in obedience trials.

HOW A DOG LEARNS

The dog is the one domestic animal that seems to want to do what his master asks. Unlike other animals that learn by fear or rewards, the dog will work willingly if he is given a kind word or a show of affection.

The hardest part of dog training is communication. If you can get across to the dog what you want him to do, he'll do it. Always remember that your dog does not understand the English language. He can, however, interpret your tone of voice and your gestures. By associating certain words with the act that accompanies them, the dog can acquire a fairly large working vocabulary. Keep in mind that it is the sound rather than the meaning of the words that the dog understands.

YOUR PART IN TRAINING

You must patiently demonstrate to your dog what each simple word of command means. Guide him with your hands and the training leash through whatever routine you are teaching him. Repeat the word associated with the act. Demonstrate again and again to give the dog the chance to make the connection in his mind. (In psychological language, you are conditioning him to give a specific response to a specific stimulus.)

Your Pom is anxious to please you. Be patient yet firm, give praise lavishly, and he will respond well to his lessons.

Once he begins to get the idea, use the word of command without any physical guidance. Drill him. When he makes mistakes, correct him, kindly at first, more severely as his training progresses.

When he does what you want, praise him lavishly with words and with pats. Don't rely on dog candy or treats in training. The dog that gets into the habit of performing for treats will seldom be fully dependable when he can't smell or see one in the offing.

THE TRAINING VOICE

When you start training your Pomeranian, use your training voice, giving commands in a firm, loud tone. Once you give the command, persist until it is obeyed even if you have to pull the dog protestingly to obey you. He must learn that training is different from playing, that a command once given must be obeyed no matter what distractions are present.

Be consistent in the use of words during training. Confine your commands to as few words as possible and never change them. It is best for only one person to carry on the dog's training because different people will use different words and tactics that will confuse the animal. The dog who hears "come," "get over here," "hurry up," "here, Rover" and other commands when he is wanted will become totally confused.

TAKE IT EASY

Training is hard on the dog — and on the trainer. A young dog just cannot take more than 10 minutes of training at a stretch, so limit the length of your first lessons. You'll find that you, too, will tend to become impatient when you stretch out a training session, and losing your temper won't help either of you. Before and after each lesson have a play period, but don't play during a training session. Even the youngest dog soon learns that schooling is a serious matter; fun comes afterward.

Don't spend too much time on one phase of training or the dog will become bored. And always try to end a training session on a pleasant note. If the dog doesn't seem to be getting what you are trying to show him, go back to something simpler that he can do. This way you will end every lesson with a pleasant feeling of accomplishment. Actually, in nine cases out of ten, if your dog isn't doing what you want, it's because you're not getting the idea over to him properly.

Teach him to sit by pulling up on the lead while pushing his hindquarters down. At the same time, give the verbal command.

It won't be long before your Pom sits every time you tell him to.

Your very young puppy should have learned to keep away from things that didn't belong to him, to be quiet when alone, to refrain from jumping on people and to walk on lead, all discussed in Chapter 5. Now that he's a little older, you are ready for his further training.

TRAINING TO SIT

Training your dog to sit should be fairly easy. Stand him on your left side, holding the lead fairly short, and command him to "Sit." As you give the verbal command, pull up slightly with the lead and push his hindquarters down (you may have to kneel to do this). Do not let him lie down or stand up. Keep him in a sitting position for a moment, then release the pressure on the lead and praise him. Your Pom, having a mind of his own, may resent being told when to sit and may put up a bit of a fuss, but don't let him get away with any nonsense. If he attempts to bite, slap him sharply across the nose. If he squirms and tries to get away, then take a few steps forward and try making him sit again. Constantly repeat the command word as you hold him in a sitting position, thus fitting the word to the action in his mind. After a while, he will begin to get the idea and will sit without your having to push his back down. When he reaches that stage, insist that he sit on command. If he is slow to obey, slap his hindquarters with the end of the lead to get him down fast. Teach him to sit on command facing you as well as when he is at your side. When he begins sitting on command with the lead on, try it with the lead off.

When he sits on command consistently, try it without the lead. A well-trained dog will sit for as long as 3 minutes with his handler out of sight.

The "lie down" is the next step in training. Have your Pom sit, then pull his front feet forward and press his shoulders down. When he gets the idea, you can just tug on the leash and give the command and hand signal.

THE "LIE DOWN"

The object of this is to get the dog to lie down either on the verbal command "Down!" or when you give him a hand signal, your hand raised, palm toward the dog — a sort of threatening gesture.

Don't start this until the dog is almost letter-perfect in sitting on command. Then, place the dog in a sit. Force him down by pulling his front feet out forward while pressing on his shoulders and repeating "Down!" Hold the dog down and stroke him gently to let him know that staying down is what you expect of him.

After he begins to get the idea, slide the lead under your left foot and give the command "Down!" At the same time, pull on the lead. This will help get the dog down. Meanwhile, raise your left hand in the down signal. Don't expect to accomplish all this in one session. Be patient and work with the dog. He'll cooperate if you show him just what you expect him to do.

THE "STAY"

The next step is to train your Pom to stay in either a "sit" or "down" position. Sit him at your side. Give him the command "Stay," but be careful not to use his name with that command as hearing his name may lead him to think that some action is expected of him. If he begins to move, repeat "Stay" firmly and hold him down in the sit. Constantly repeat the word "stay" to fix the meaning of that command in his mind. When he stays for a short time, gradually increase the length of his stay. The hand signal for "stay" is a downward sweep of your hand toward the dog's nose, with the palm toward him. While he is sitting, walk around him and stand in front of him. Hold the lead at first; later, drop the lead on the ground in front of him and keep him sitting. If he bolts, correct him severely and force him back to a sit in the same place.

To get him to stay, sweep your hand down with your palm toward him.

If your dog begins to move during the "stay," repeat the command firmly and give the hand signal again.

Use some word such as "okay" or "up" to let him know when he can get up, and praise him well for a good performance. As this practice continues, walk farther and farther away from him. Later, try sitting him, giving him the command to stay, and then walk out of sight, first for a few seconds, then for longer periods. A well-trained dog should stay where you put him without moving for three minutes or more.

Similarly, practice having him stay in down position, first with you near him, later when you step out of sight.

THE "COME" ON COMMAND

A young puppy will come a-running to people, but an older puppy or dog will have other plans of his own when his master calls him. However, you can train your Pom to come when you call him if you begin when he is young. At first, work with him on lead. Sit the dog, then back away the length of the lead and call him, putting as much coaxing affection in your voice as possible. Give an easy tug on the lead to get him started. When he does come, make a big fuss over him and it might help to hand him a piece of dog candy or food as a reward. He should get the idea soon. Then attach a long piece of cord to the lead — 15 or 20 feet — and make him come to you from that distance. When he's coming pretty consistently, have him sit when he reaches you.

Don't be too eager to practice coming on command off lead. Wait till you are certain that you have the dog under perfect control before you try calling him when he's free. Once he gets the idea that he can disobey a command to come and get away with it, your training program will suffer a serious setback. Keep in mind that your dog's life may depend on his immediate response to a command to come when he is called. If he disobeys off lead, put the collar back on and correct him severely with jerks of the lead. He'll get the idea.

In training your dog to come, never use the command when you want to punish him. He should associate the "come" with something pleasant. If he comes very slowly, you can speed his response by pulling on the lead, calling him and running backward with him at a brisk pace.

At first, practice the "sit," "down," "stay" and "come" indoors; then try it in an outdoor area where there are distractions to show the dog that he must obey under any conditions.

Soon your Pom will stay absolutely still, standing, sitting or lying down, until you give the okay to move.

Here the Pom is just getting used to the lead. Soon he should be heeling, walking at your left knee and adjusting his pace to yours.

HEELING

"Heeling" in dog language means having your pet walk alongside you on your left side, close to your left leg, on lead or off. With patience and effort you can train your Pom to walk with you even on a crowded street or in the presence of other dogs. However, don't begin this part of his training too early. Normally a dog much under six months old is just too young to absorb the idea of heeling.

For training him to heel, you may have to substitute a metal-link "choke" collar for the nylon lead that you have been using. Be certain to learn the correct way to put on this collar so that the loop which attaches to the lead goes *over*, not *under* the dog's neck. When you jerk on the lead it will tighten, when you release pressure it will loosen. The collar should be big enough to dangle a few inches. For training purposes a 6-foot webbed cloth lead is best.

With enough repetition, your dog will associate the word "heel" with your desire to have him at your left leg. The tool for this part of the training is the lead and collar, assisted by your verbal commands.

Put the dog at your left side, sitting. Then say "heel" loudly and start walking at a brisk pace. Do not pull the dog with you, but guide him by tugs at the lead. Keep some slack on the lead and use your left hand to snap the lead for a correction. Always start off with your left foot and after a while the dog will learn to watch that foot and follow it. Keep repeating "heel" as you walk, snapping the dog back into position if he lags behind or forges ahead. If he gets out of control, reverse your course sharply and snap him along after you. Keep up a running conversation with your dog, telling him what a good fellow he is when he is heeling, letting him know when he is not.

At first limit your heeling practice to about 5 minutes at a time; later extend it to 15 minutes or a half-hour. To keep your dog interested, vary the routine. Make right and left turns, change your pace from a normal walk to a fast trot to a very slow walk. Occasionally make a sharp about-face.

Remember to emphasize the word "heel" throughout this practice and to use your voice to let him know that you are displeased when he goes ahead or drops behind or swings wide.

If you are handling him properly, the Pom should begin to get the idea of heeling in about 15 minutes. If you get no response whatever, if the dog runs away from you, fights the lead, gets you and himself tangled in the lead, it may indicate that he is still young, or that you aren't showing him what you expect him to do.

Practicing 15 minutes a day, in 6 or 7 weeks your Pom should have developed to the stage where you can remove the lead and he'll heel along-side you. First try throwing the lead over your shoulder or fastening it to your belt, or remove the lead and tie a piece of thin cord (fishing line will do nicely) to his collar. Then try him off lead. Keep his attention by constantly talking; slap your left leg to keep his attention on you. If he breaks away, return to the collar and lead treatment for a while.

"HEEL" MEANS SIT, TOO

To the dog, the command "Heel" will also mean that he has to sit in heel position at your left side when you stop walking — with no additional command from you. As you practice heeling, force him to sit whenever you stop, at first using the word "sit," then switching over to the command "heel." He'll soon get the idea and plop his rear end down when you stop and wait for you to give the command "heel" and start walking again.

TEACHING TO COME TO HEEL

The object of this is for you to stand still, say "Heel!" and have your dog come right over to you and sit by your left knee in heel position. If your dog has been trained to sit without command every time you stop, he's ready for this step.

Sit him in front of and facing you and step back a few feet. Say "Heel" in your most commanding tone of voice and pull the dog into heel position,

Don't overwork your dog—or yourself—during training sessions. Take time out for relaxation and play.

making him sit. There are several different ways to do this. You can swing the dog around behind you from your right side, behind your back and to heel position. Or you can pull him toward you, keep him on your left side and swing him to heel position. Use your left heel to straighten him out if he begins to sit behind you or crookedly. This may take a little work, but the dog will get the idea if you show him just what you want.

THE "STAND"

Your Pomeranian should be trained to stand on one spot without moving his feet, and should allow a stranger to run his hands over his body and legs without showing any resentment or fear. Use the same method you used in training him to stay on the sit and down. While walking, place your left hand out, palm toward his nose, and command him to stay. His first impulse will be to sit, so be prepared to stop that by placing your hand under his body. If he's really stubborn, you may have to wrap the lead around his body near his hindquarters and hold him up until he gets the idea that this is different from the command to sit. Praise him for standing and walk to the end of the lead. Correct him strongly if he starts to move. Have a stranger approach him and run his hands over the dog's back and down his legs. Keep him standing until you come back to him. Walk around him from his left side, come to heel position, and let the dog sit as you praise him lavishly.

Don't expect to accomplish all the training overnight. Generally a dog-training school will devote about ten weeks, with one session a week, to all this training. Between lessons the dogs and their masters are expected to work about fifteen minutes every day on the exercises.

If you'd like more detailed information on training your dog, you'll find it in the pages of HOW TO HOUSEBREAK AND TRAIN YOUR DOG.

There are dog-training classes in all parts of the country, some sponsored by the local A.S.P.C.A. A free list of dog-training clubs and schools is available from the Gaines Dog Research Center, 250 Park Avenue, New York, New York.

If you feel that you lack the time or the skill to train your dog yourself, there are professional dog trainers who will do it for you, but basically dog training is a matter of training *you* and your dog to work together as a team, and if you don't do it yourself you will miss a lot of fun.

The most important part of training is the praise you give your dog when he has learned his lesson.

ADVANCED TRAINING AND OBEDIENCE TRIALS

In recent years, many Pomeranian owners have found that their dogs show considerable aptitude for advanced obedience training and the number of Poms entered in obedience trials at A.K.C. shows has been increasing. Most dog shows now include obedience classes at which your dog can qualify for his "degrees" to demonstrate his usefulness as a companion dog, not merely as a pet or show dog.

The A.K.C. obedience trials are divided into three classes: Novice, Open and Utility.

In the Novice Class, the dog will be judged on the following basis:

Test	Maximum Score
Heel on leash	35
Stand for examination by judge	30
Heel free — off leash	45
Recall (come on command)	30
1-minute sit (handler in ring)	30
3-minute down (handler in ring)	30
Maximum total score	200

If the dog "qualifies" in three different shows by earning at least 50 per cent of the points for each test, with a total of at least 170 for the trial, he has earned the Companion Dog degree and the letters C.D. are entered in the stud book after his name.

After the dog has qualified as a C.D., he is eligible to enter the Open Class competition where he will be judged on this basis:

Test	Maximum Score
Heel free	40
Drop on recall	30
Retrieve (wooden dumbell) on flat	25
Broad jump	20
3-minute sit (handler out of ring)	25
5-minute down (handler out of ring)	25
Maximum total score	200

Again he must qualify in three shows for the C.D.X. (Companion Dog Excellent) title and then is eligible for the Utility Class where he can earn the Utility Dog degree in these rugged tests:

Test	Maximum Score
Scent discrimination (picking up article handled by master from group of articles) — Article #1	20
Scent discrimination — Article #2	20

Scent discrimination — Article #3............................	20
Seek back (picking up article dropped by handler)....	30
Signal exercise (heeling, etc., on hand signal only)....	35
Directed jumping (over hurdle and bar jump)..........	40
Group examination	35
Maximum total score...	200

For more complete information about these obedience trials, write to the American Kennel Club, 221 Fourth Avenue, New York 3, N. Y., and ask for their free booklet "Regulations and Standards for Obedience Trials." Spayed females and dogs that are disqualified from breed shows because of physical defects (see the Standards in Chapter 1) are eligible to compete in these trials.

Besides the formal A.K.C. obedience trials, there are informal "match" shows in which dogs compete for ribbons and inexpensive trophies. These shows are run by local Pomeranian clubs and by all-breed obedience clubs, and in many localities the A.S.P.C.A. and other groups conduct their own obedience shows. Your local pet shop or kennel can keep you informed about such shows in your vicinity and you will find them listed in the different dog magazines or in the pet column of your local paper.

7. Showing Your Pomeranian

You probably think that your Pomeranian is the best in the country and possibly in the world, but before you enter the highly competitive world of the show, get some unbiased expert opinions. Compare your dog against standards on pages 8-10. If a Pomeranian club in your vicinity is holding a match show, enter your dog and see what the judges think of him. If he places in a few match shows, then you might begin seriously considering the big-time shows. Visit a few as a spectator first and make careful mental notes of what is required of the handlers and the dogs. Watch how the experienced handlers manage their dogs to bring out their best points. See how they use pieces of liver to "bait" the dogs and keep them alert in the ring. If experts think your dog has the qualities to make him a champion, you might want to hire a professional handler to show him.

WHAT THE JUDGE LOOKS FOR

In addition to comparing the dog with the standard for the breed, the judge will look for spirit and soundness. In the matter of size, some years ago judges were inclined to give the nod to smaller Poms in the 2-pound range, but today's judges are more likely to choose a more soundly built Pom weighing between 4 and 5 pounds.

The strutting gait of the Pom is one of his most attractive features. Besides showing the animal's spirit, the manner in which your Pom travels around the ring indicates to the experienced eye much about the dog's conformation. The show pose of the Pom is designed to show his best features. While the experienced and professional handler knows how to pose the dog to show his best points and hide any minor faults, most judges know these fine "tricks" too and concentrate on the dog itself rather than the way he is being shown.

Once beyond the puppy class, the trim is extremely important. It should be done by an expert, but not too close to the day of the show. It's hard to fool a judge by trimming the Pom to conceal faults. Some exhibitors will try to disguise a low-set tail by trimming around its base. Others will take too much hair from the ears to make them appear smaller, and some even clip the muzzles to give the desired "wedgie" shape.

If you plan to show your Pom, you'll need a carrying case for his trips. One of the Pom's advantages is that he can be taken everywhere so easily.

The Pom's facial expression is another point that judges weigh heavily. He should have a sweet, friendly expression. Small ears, closely set, a wedge-shaped muzzle and strong legs are musts for a winning dog.

HOW TO ENTER

If your dog is purebred and registered with the American Kennel Club— or eligible for registration — you may enter him in the appropriate show class for which his age, sex and previous show record qualify him. You will find coming shows listed in the different dog magazines and in the "Pomeranian Review" (James K. Arima, editor, Ridge Drive, Glen Hills, Rockville, Maryland). Write to the secretary of the show, asking for the "Premium List." When you receive the entry form, fill it in carefully and send it back with the required entry fee. Then, before the show, you'll receive your Exhibitor's Pass which will admit you and your dog to the show.

If you have followed the regular grooming routine, the Pom won't need much special care before the show. When you brush him, don't flatten his hair; let it stand out from his body.

Here are the five official show classes:

Puppy Class: Open to dogs at least 6 months and not more than 12 months of age. Limited to dogs whelped in the United States and Canada.

Novice Class: Open to dogs 6 months of age or older that have never won a first prize at a show — wins in puppy class excepted. Limited to dogs whelped in the United States or Canada.

Bred by Exhibitor Class: Open to all dogs except champions 6 months of age or over who are exhibited by the same person or kennel who was the recognized breeder on the records of the American Kennel Club.

American-Bred Class: Open to dogs that are not champions, 6 months of age or over, whelped in the United States after a mating which took place in the United States.

Open Class: Open to dogs 6 months of age or over, with no exceptions. In addition there are local classes, "special classes" and brace entries.

HOW THE SHOW WORKS

Separate classes are held for males and females and four places are awarded in each class. The male and female that win a first place in any class are qualified for the Winners Class which is also divided by sex.

Now it gets complicated. Assume that you have a male Pom entered in the Puppy Class. He competes against other male puppies; meanwhile the female Poms in the Puppy Class are competing against each other. He wins first place in his Puppy Class, then competes against the winning males in the other classes. Here he gets the nod again and is now Winners Dog. Then, he earns a number of points towards his championship depending on the number of entries and other factors — just too complicated to go into here — but winning 15 points makes him a champion.

Next step is appearing in the ring against the Winners Bitch for the title Best of Winners. Then he may still have to face Pom champions who were entered in the Specials Class for the Best of Breed. Still tops, he goes against the winners in other toy dog classifications for Best of Group and finally meets the winners of other groups for the coveted Best in Show — the top dog of the show.

For full information on the dog show rules, write to the American Kennel Club, 221 Fourth Avenue, New York 3, N. Y. Ask for the free booklet, "Rules Applying to Registration and Dog Shows."

Have his hair trimmed, give him a manicure, and he's ready to prance around the show ring.

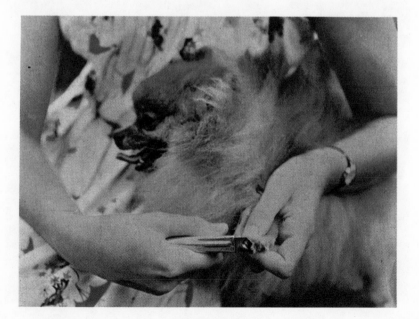

ADVANCE PREPARATION

Before you go to a show your dog should be trained to gait at a trot beside you, with head up and in a straight line. In the ring you will have to gait around the edge with other dogs and then individually up and down the center runner. In addition the dog must stand for examination by the judge, who will look at him closely and feel his head and body structure. He should be taught to stand squarely, hind feet slightly back, head up on the alert. He must hold the pose when you place his feet and show animation for a piece of boiled liver in your hand or a toy mouse thrown in front of you.

The show may bring a day of triumph to both of you, complete with trophies, ribbons and the magic letters "Ch." before your dog's name.

Showing requires practice training sessions in advance. Get a friend to act as judge and set the dog up and "show" him for a few minutes every day.

If you have carefully followed the daily and weekly grooming routine, your Pom should need little more than the expert trim for his show appearance.

The day before the show, pack your kit. You will want to take a water dish and bottle of water for your dog (so that he won't be affected by a change in drinking water, and you won't have to go look for it). Take the show lead, the grooming tools and the identification ticket sent by the show superintendent, noting the time you must be there and the place where the show will be held, as well as the time of judging.

THE DAY OF THE SHOW

Don't feed your dog the morning of the show, or give him at most a light meal. He will be more comfortable in the car on the way, and will show more enthusiastically. When you arrive at the show grounds an official veterinarian will check your dog for health, and then you should find his bench and settle him there. Locate the ring where Pomeranians will be judged, take the dog to the exercise ring to relieve himself, and give him a small drink of water. After a final grooming, you have only to wait until your class is called. It is your responsibility to be at the ring at the proper time.

Then, as you step into the ring, try to keep your knees from rattling too loudly. Before you realize it you'll be out again, perhaps back with the winners for more judging and finally — with luck — it will be all over and you'll have a ribbon and an armful of silver trophies. And a very wonderful dog!

8. Caring for the Female and Raising Puppies

Whether or not you bought your female dog intending to breed her, some preparation is necessary when and if you decide to take this step.

WHEN TO BREED

It is usually best to breed on the second or third season. Plan in advance the time of year which is best for you, taking into account where the puppies will be born and raised. You will keep them until they are at least six weeks old, and a litter of frisky pups takes up considerable space by then. Other considerations are selling the puppies (Christmas vs. springtime sales), your own vacation, and time available to care for them. You'll need at least an hour a day to feed and clean up after the mother and puppies but probably it will take you much longer—with time out to admire and play with them!

CHOOSING THE STUD

You can plan to breed your female about 6½ months after the start of her last season, although a variation of a month or two either way is not unusual. Choose the stud dog and make arrangements well in advance. If you are breeding for show stock, which may command better prices, a mate should be chosen with an eye to complementing the deficiencies of your female. If possible, they should have several ancestors in common within the last two or three generations, as such combinations generally "click" best. He should have a good show record or be the sire of show winners if old enough to be proven.

The owner of such a male usually charges a fee for the use of the dog. The fee varies. This does not guarantee a litter, but you generally have the right to breed your female again if she does not have puppies. In some cases the owner of the stud will agree to take a choice puppy in place of a stud fee. You should settle all details beforehand, including the possibility of a single surviving puppy, deciding the age at which he is to make his choice and take the pup, and so on.

If you want to raise a litter "just for the fun of it" and plan merely to make use of an available male Pomeranian, the most important point is temperament. Make sure the dog is friendly as well as healthy, because a bad disposition could appear in his puppies, and this is the worst of all traits in a dog destined to be a pet. In such cases a "stud fee puppy," not necessarily the choice of the litter, is the usual payment.

PREPARATION FOR BREEDING

Before you breed your female, make sure she is in good health. She should be neither too thin nor too fat. Any skin disease *must* be cured, before it can be passed on to the puppies. If she has worms she should be wormed before being bred or within three weeks afterward. It is generally considered a good idea to revaccinate her against distemper and hepatitis before the puppies are born. This will increase the immunity the puppies receive during their early, most vulnerable period.

The female will probably be ready to breed 12 days after the first colored discharge. You can usually make arrangements to board her with

If you're breeding your Pom for show stock, the mate should have good bloodlines and several ancestors in common. If you want puppies just for fun, good health and a good disposition are the most important traits in a mate.

the owner of the male for a few days, to insure her being there at the proper time, or you can take her to be mated and bring her home the same day. If she still appears receptive she may be bred again two days later. However, some females never show signs of willingness, so it helps to have the experience of a breeder. Usually the second day after the discharge changes color is the proper time, and she may be bred for about three days following. For an additional week or so she may have some discharge and attract other dogs by her odor, but can seldom be bred.

THE FEMALE IN WHELP

You can expect the puppies nine weeks from the day of breeding, although 61 days is as common as 63. During this time the female should receive normal care and exercise. If she was overweight, don't increase her food at first; excess weight at whelping time is bad. If she is on the thin side build her up, giving some soup and biscuit at noon if she likes it. You may add one of the mineral and vitamin supplements to her food, to make sure that the puppies will be healthy. As her appetite increases, feed her more. During the last two weeks the puppies grow enormously and she will probably have little room for food and less appetite. She should be tempted with meat, however.

As the female in whelp grows heavier, cut out violent exercise and jumping. Although a dog used to such activities will often play with the children or run around voluntarily, restrain her for her own sake.

PREPARING FOR THE PUPPIES

Prepare a whelping box a few days before the puppies are due, and allow the mother to sleep there overnight or to spend some time in it during the day to become accustomed to it. Then she is less likely to try to have her pups under the front porch or in the middle of your bed.

Layers of newspaper spread over the whole area will make excellent bedding and be absorbent enough to keep the surface warm and dry. They should be removed daily and replaced with another thick layer. An old quilt or washable blanket makes better footing for the nursing puppies than slippery newspaper during the first week, and is softer for the mother.

Be prepared for the actual whelping several days in advance. Usually the female will tear up papers, refuse food and generally act restless. These may be false alarms; the real test is her temperature, which will drop to below 100° about 12 hours before whelping. Take it with a rectal thermometer morning and evening, and put her in the pen, looking in on her frequently, when the temperature goes down.

WHELPING .

Usually little help is needed but it is wise to stay close to make sure that the mother's lack of experience does not cause an unnecessary accident. Be ready to help when the first puppy arrives, for it could smother if she does not break the membrane enclosing it. She should start right away to lick the puppy, drying and stimulating it, but you can do it with a soft rough towel, instead. The afterbirth should follow the birth of each puppy, attached to the puppy by the long umbilical cord. Watch to make sure that each is expelled, anyway, for retaining this material can cause infection. In her instinct for cleanliness the mother will probably eat the afterbirth after biting the cord. One or two will not hurt her; they stimulate milk supply as well as labor for remaining pups. But too many can make her lose appetite for the food she needs to feed her pups and regain her strength. So remove the rest of them along with the wet newspapers and keep the pen dry and clean to relieve her anxiety.

If the mother does not bite the cord, or does it too close to the body, take over the job, to prevent an umbilical hernia. Tearing is recommended, but you can cut it, about two inches from the body, with a sawing motion of scissors, sterilized in alcohol. Then dip the end in a shallow dish of iodine; the cord will dry up and fall off in a few days.

The puppies should follow each other at intervals of not more than half an hour. If more times goes past and you are sure there are still pups to come, a brisk walk outside may start labor again. If she is actively straining without producing a puppy it may be presented backward, a so-called "breech" or upside down birth. Careful assistance with a well-soaped finger to feel for the puppy or ease it back may help, but never attempt to pull it by force against the mother. This could cause serious damage, so let an expert handle it.

If anything seems wrong, waste no time in calling your veterinarian, who can examine her and if necessary give hormones which will bring the remaining puppies. You may want his experience in whelping the litter even if all goes well. He will probably prefer to have the puppies born at his hospital rather than to get up in the middle of the night to come to your home. The mother would, no doubt, prefer to stay at home, but you can be sure she will get the best of care in his hospital. If the puppies are born at home and all goes as it should, watch the mother carefully afterward.

RAISING THE PUPPIES

Hold each puppy to a breast as soon as he is dry, for a good meal without competition. Then he may join his littermates in the basket, out of his mother's way while she is whelping. Keep a supply of evaporated milk on hand for emergencies, or later weaning. A formula of evaporated milk, corn syrup and a little water with egg yolk should be warmed and fed in a doll or baby bottle if necessary. A supplementary feeding often helps weak pups over the hump. Keep track of birth weights, and take weekly readings; it will furnish an accurate record of the pups' growth and health.

After the puppies have arrived, take the mother outside for a walk and drink, and then leave her to take care of them. She will probably not want to stay away more than a minute or two for the first few weeks. Be sure to keep water available at all times, and feed her milk or broth frequently, as she needs liquids to produce milk. Encourage her to eat, with her favorite foods, until she asks for it of her own accord. She will soon develop a ravenous appetite and should have at least two large meals a day, with dry food available in addition.

Prepare a warm place to put the puppies after they are born to keep them dry and help them to a good start in life. An electric heating pad or hot water bottle covered with flannel in the bottom of a cardboard box should be set near the mother so that she can see her puppies. She will usually allow you to help, but don't take the puppies out of sight, and let her handle things if your interference seems to make her nervous.

Be sure that all the puppies are getting enough to eat. If the mother sits or stands, instead of lying still to nurse, the probable cause is scratching from the puppies' nails. You can remedy this by clipping them, as you do hers. Manicure scissors will do for these tiny claws.

Some breeders advise disposing of the smaller or weaker pups in a large litter, as the mother has trouble in handling more than six or seven. But you can help her out by preparing an extra puppy box or basket. Leave half the litter with the mother and the other half in a warm place, changing off at two hour intervals at first. Later you may change them less frequently, leaving them all together except during the day. Try supplementary feeding, too; as soon as their eyes open, at about two weeks, they will lap from a dish, anyway.

WEANING THE PUPPIES

The puppies should normally be completely weaned at five weeks, although you start to feed them at three weeks. They will find it easier to lap semi-solid food. At four weeks they will eat four meals a day, and soon do without their mother entirely. Start them on mixed dog food, or leave it with them in a dish for self-feeding. Don't leave water with them all the time; at this age everything is to play with and they will use it as a wading pool. They can drink all they need if it is offered several times a day, after meals.

As the puppies grow up the mother will go into the pen only to nurse them, first sitting up and then standing. To dry her up completely, keep the mother away for longer periods; after a few days of part-time nursing she can stay away for longer periods, and then completely. The little milk left will be resorbed.

The puppies may be put outside, unless it is too cold, as soon as their eyes are open, and will benefit from the sunlight and vitamins. A rubber mat or newspapers underneath will protect them from cold or damp.

You can expect the pups to need at least one worming before they are ready to go to new homes, so take a stool sample to your veterinarian before they are three weeks old. If one puppy has worms all should be wormed. Follow the veterinarian's advice, and this applies also to vaccination. If you plan to keep a pup you will want to vaccinate him at the earliest age, so his littermates should be done at the same time.